on the
PURSUIT
of
IMPROVEMENT

FOR ORGANIZATIONS, GROUPS, AND YOU

TOM J. GEORGE

On the Pursuit of Improvement:
For Organizations, Groups, and You
© 2024 Tom J. George

ISBN: 978-1-7338972-6-6

Available on Amazon.com

Production services:
Populore Publishing Company
Morgantown, West Virginia

In Memory of My Aunts
Misses Sarah, Eva, and Mary George
&
Miss Ellen David

"We but mirror the world. ... If we could change ourselves, the tendencies in the world would also change. ... This is the divine mystery supreme. A wonderful thing it is and the source of our happiness. We need not wait to see what others do."
— Mahatma Gandhi

CONTENTS

Introduction

Is pursuing improvement important? Striving for continual betterment is essential to build strong relationships, set boundaries, form closer bonds, aid awareness, and assist purposefulness. In this volume, drawing from my own experiences, research, and insights, pragmatic points for how to go about this pursuit are presented. This includes a three-point model for improvement and nine basic skills *all* need (and a structure for practicing them in groups). Also, the importance of considering organizational structures, individual personalities, and the values held by both groups and individuals is explained.

Early in my engineering career, I admired William Edwards Deming (1900–1993). In 1947 he was a consultant to the US government to support Japan's recovery from WWII. He impressed his Japanese government hosts, and as such, he was requested to present his improvement theories to their business leaders. Deming summarized his approach with "14 Points." Desperate to be commercially competitive, Japan seized Deming's approach to assure quality products. Japan's subsequent success in the marketplace popularized the Total Quality Management (TQM) movement, boosting the quality of manufactured products worldwide.

Ultimate Model? Deming's fourteen-point improvement model was a challenge for me to memorize. Observing quality-improvement consultants shrink Deming's points from fourteen to as few as five to seven points, I reached for even more simplification. Over several years, I evolved a three-point summary to embody the key improvement elements important for highest quality results: *Vision, Plan, Communication.* Years of quietly self-testing gave me confidence in the validity of this elegantly, at least to me, simplified three-point *model for improvement.* Engaged in creating or executing a project, using my "insightful three," I would inquire: "Do we have a *vision?* Do we have a *plan?* Is *communication* receiving appropriate emphasis?" Frequently, all three were deficient, requiring a better vision, a clearer plan, and much improved communication.

Do my three fundamental points represent the ultimate model for improvement, for project success? Researching, I found competing models such as "Act-Plan-Study-Do" and a spin-off, "Act-Plan-Do-Check." Other approaches promote "Identify-Plan-Execute-Review" and "Commitment-Strategy-Process-Performance." This one, with quite a long name, recommends steps for continuous improvement: "Making Problems Visible, Developing Countermeasure, Determining Root Cause, Hypothesizing Solution, Testing Hypothesis, and Implement Solution." I found all of these examples simply by an internet search using the two words *improvement* and *models*, and scrolling through the search results.

Whether it's mine, or one of the innumerable alternative models for improvement, we each would be wise to select one and use it as a tool to aid our being attuned to the significance of improving processes and results and to the concept of continual improvement. Searching many years for an easier-to-remember, perhaps superior, model, I finally developed my own (vision, plan, communication). One example of arriving at—and using—a model for a specific context is given in Chapter 5, when I discuss the church as a sort of case study.* Another insight this research gave me was that we should reach for perfection while realizing that obtaining it is most probably impossible.

Beyond Models. An improvement tool is important. However, attentiveness to our organizational environment is often more so. Simplifying, we live in a world of either *participative (democratic)* or *autocratic* organizational climates. Sometimes we face a confusing mixture of these. Both environments are valid. Autocratic "top down" is vital in a wartime battlefield situation; or, whenever a situation is urgently serious. But, most problem-solving climates are not crisis bound, and thus, they deserve the opportunity for deliberative participative activity. In autocratic circumstances, one usually can employ participative activities but must doubly ensure permission is granted and that all of the autocratic communication processes are respected. Chapter 3 is dedicated to exploring the importance of organizational structure, particularly the tension between autocratic and democratic models.

Foundational leader skills are critical for all. To maximize success, implementing a model for improvement is aided by skilled leaders, but also, by followers who appreciate the basic skills required of leadership. To my considerable surprise, in my search for *basic* leader skills, they ("short-listed") were not clearly obvious. I was confronted by authors or training businesses suggesting various numbers of "key" skills for leaders. Furthermore, the conflicting terminology used to define specific skills confused me. Therefore, I spent months researching and documenting all leader skills that "experts" suggested as essential.

Starting with multiple lists of conflicting suggestions, I labored at consolidating proclaimed "leader skills" into the most basic few. My goal was a one-word descriptor for each basic skill. In three cases, two-word descriptors were needed. I arrived at nine leader skill categories as follows: 1) Building Teams, 2) Motivating,

---

* This book is not a "religious work." Rather, I use a few church experiences as examples to help me anchor my secular model for improvement. —TJG

3) Delegating, 4) Facilitating, 5) Giving Feedback, 6) Listening, 7) Mentoring, 8) Planning, and 9) Critical Thinking. Perhaps in time, a competent authority will improve my nomenclature and/or the number of true "basic" leader skills.

I searched for a training consultant to build a training offering specific to instilling all of these skills under one umbrella event (course, seminar, or program). Unable to identify such an expert, I decided I must develop such lesson plans. What I developed for leader skill training is presented in Chapter 2, *Lesson Plans for Basic Leader/Follower Skills*. I'm confident that over time my proposed skill training and its delivery will be continually improved, especially through others' feedback. Indeed, sharing my leader training ideas has resulted in affirming feedback from Waynesburg University (WU) in Pennsylvania, which is bringing my concepts to the classroom. Founded in 1849, with an emphasis on imparting religion, morality, and knowledge,[†] WU is giving greater import to training to introduce skills, as, for example, suggested in Chapter 2. In a full semester offering, students are now engaged in leader skill training without neglecting the importance of knowledge-based educational content.

Why are these skills important for followers too? I believe that followers should possess—or, at least be attuned to—the nine basic leader skills. Such competency and sensitivity is needed to be a worthy follower. And, equally important, it's needed to be prepared to lead when called. This leadership might be in a specific role such as a parent or manager. But it could also be in response to a "call"—that began as a nudge or with a question.

Biblical input I received from a learned priest many years ago caused me to consider how best to acquire leader skills. Back then, in my church, I was frustrated by the lack of interest in lay leadership. Making numerous inquiries, it was suggested that I have a talk with a Biblical scholar, Fr. Jack Norman Sparks. At the visit, within minutes, this priest—and author, mentor, and Biblical

---

† *Against All Odds, The Story of Waynesburg University's Remarkable Transition,* by James K. Dittmar, PhD, The Donning Company Publishers, 2010.

scholar—directed me to read a Biblical passage. The passage made clear, at least to me, that not a few, but all Christians are individually obligated to be leaders. Since then, I've been driven to ascertain and critically consider the requirements of leadership. The Bible passage about all Christians being leaders is cited in Chapter 5.

What about communication skills? "Communication" is not listed as a basic skill for leaders because it represents a complex and rich ability with many facets, including being the foundation and beneficiary of all nine basic leader skills. Perhaps communication is the most essential human ability. Within Chapter 2's lesson plans for basic leader/follower skills, in the activities for each, communication is practiced. Effective communication involves—among so many other capabilities—verbal expression, non-verbal cues, presentation competence, cultural awareness, and a sound value system.

Of my nine basic skills, my life experience suggests that the most important communication-related skill is listening. And, it's the most frequently called upon. To enhance listening, my favorite tool is to ask a good question, shut up, and truly *listen*. This is not easy. I've discovered my best moments of communication come when I practice active listening.

In my faith, partaking in Communion is a central belief. I'm still researching, but my impression of its purpose is shifting. Whereas I had, first and foremost, believed it a personal event for my redemption, I'm suspecting its purpose for the early church was for Christians to come together as a community and *listen* (to each other)—as brothers and sisters in Christ.

Training for the basic skills. Unable to identify training lesson plans for my nine basic leader/follower skills or a consultant to develop them, my recourse was to create them myself. I wrongly thought that I could do it rather quickly. Finding sources and guidance for developing the lesson plans' content took several weeks. With the structure and format of the plans established, it then took several months to produce them, as presented in Chapter 2. Hopefully, over time they will be affirmed and improved. Recent news is encouraging. Waynesburg University has reviewed the nine basic skills proposed and will use them as the foundation to create a pioneering semester-long (fifteen weeks) course to instill the skills and impart related knowledge.

My desire is that users of this barely book-length volume come to appreciate for themselves the importance of continuous improvement. I hope that those who read this book and participate in the training exercises proposed (both trainers and trainees) will critically reflect on both the models of improvement and key qualities of leaders and followers presented here. By engaging these ideas with care and consideration, users will be able to evaluate, adapt, own, and—of course—improve these concepts so that they become seamlessly incorporated into their life pursuits.

"I define a leader as anyone who takes responsibility for finding the potential in people and processes, and who has the courage to develop that potential."
—Brené Brown

CHAPTER 1

Ultimate Model for Improvement?

An essential marker of our humanity is our perpetual curiosity. Inquisitiveness is necessary for physical, cognitive, and social/emotional development, but to different degrees in each of us. In the beginning, all of my childhood friends liked playing with simple wooden blocks. Soon I found myself moving on to a more complex construction toy: an Erector Set. Initially, friends would join me as I made model vehicles and structures, with metal pieces joined with tiny nuts and bolts. Soon, though, I looked up and wondered, "Where did my friends go?" My greater interest was building even more complex Gilbert Erector Set projects. Playing outside with friends was secondary.

In engineering school, many students did as well or better than I on standard tests that pressed one's ability to memorize. However, I greatly exceeded my student competitors at complex problem solving. I was evidently more curious, and I was patient to arrive at the solution. In work as a graduate engineer, Dr. Deming's gift of the "14 Points" for improvement intrigued me. However, the challenge of memorizing all those points articulated in lengthy statements caused me to crave something simpler. My spirit of inquiry made me attentive to competing improvement consultants who proposed simpler models with five to seven points. Even these taxed my memory. Thus, began the arduous but enjoyable challenge to simplify. Over many years I revisited this challenge. One day I arrived at the eventual truth that all other points proposed could be folded into three one-word ideas:

- Vision
- Plan
- Communication

Should I rejoice, celebrate, brag, and perhaps, publish? I thought it best to quietly test them. So, over the years, I did so on any project of interest. I did so for many activities, whether they be on the job, in my family life, or at church. I tested my three-point model by asking for clarification of the vision and the plan; and, if they weren't apparent, I would inquire regarding the communication processes to be used in obtaining and clearly defining the vision and plan.

Vision

Too often, we embark upon a venture with a foggy notion of the most desired outcome. For any worthy project, the clearer the vision of outcome, the more likely achieving it. The vision should be in writing—a vision statement. Its cornerstone is the plan, but the more strategic its structure, the better. And, clearly categorizing and stating our plan's sub-goal(s) makes it easier to motivate participants striving to help achieve them. Our vision consolidates effort that unites people to improve overall productive efficiencies, and it helps existing and potential participants more clearly differentiate their effort from competing activities. A strong vision brings people on board and strengthens commitment.

An outstanding vision statement is concise, inspiring, clear, future oriented, challenging, and stable. Being stable, it imbues a long-term commitment to avoid giving participants the impression that this vision will be another annoying passing fad or simply the result of quick, careless brainstorming.

A vision statement shares a high-level idealistic view of the activities in which participants will engage for the emotional satisfaction of achieving group success, while buoyed and encouraged by the excitement of "teaming." In autocratic organizations, it is more challenging to have a vision statement feel shared. Why? Participative organizations engage their members in writing the statement, but autocratic organizations tend to set the vision from above with little or no input from below. Even autocratic leaders are wise to consider input from subordinates as it increases their buy-in.

Plan

The plan summarizes key activities for establishing the scope of an undertaking. It carefully identifies and articulates each task necessary to reach the overall final objective—the vision. The plan should also describe the relationship (or lack of connection) between each task, including scheduling information (start, sequence, stop times, staffing, funding, etc.). A flawed plan or no serious planning increases the probability of failure of a project, program, or enterprise. For more complicated projects, early in my engineering career, I adopted the Critical Path Method (CPM). The chart on the following page is a simplified illustration of the CPM approach.

Communication

To illustrate the importance of good communication, I will share some incidents from my life.

Completing a mechanical engineering degree, I entered the US Navy. My assignment upon graduating from Officer Candidate School (OCS) was US destroyer duty. Though designated an engineering duty officer (EDO), my fellow warship officers were unaware my designation differed from their "line officer" appointments. My designation was uncommon in the destroyer Navy.

By coincidence, my personality differed from the line officers, as I wasn't inclined to bark orders. In my normal Engineering

Critical Path Method, Simplified: Making Breakfast

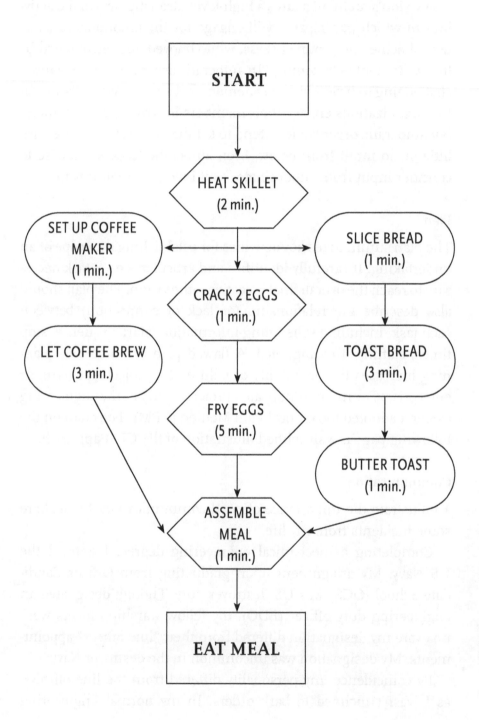

Department responsibilities, I minimized autocratic ordering, realizing listening was best for overseeing and inspiring excellent ship maintenance. I rarely growled an order, and did so only when necessary for appearance's sake. My innate skill and personality paid off. When rated by special external reviews, our Engineering Department jumped from its usual last place to first place. Thus, my higher ranked officers were disappointed when I was, at my own quiet request, suddenly transferred to Navy repair shipyard duty. Having learned all I could pretending to be a line officer, I had requested the transfer.

Still an EDO, at the shipyard I assumed an additional title, ship superintendent. As such, I was one of a very few officers in a group overseeing ship construction and overhaul projects in the Philadelphia Naval Shipyard in eastern Pennsylvania. In hindsight, it was due to strong listening skills that my ship construction and testing-at-sea projects succeeded on schedule whereas, too often, others' slipped completion dates.

My shipyard interfaces were predominantly with civilian workers. Instead of flaunting superiority, I continued with my engrained listening style. I respected all staff assigned to my upgrade and repair projects—from highest ranking civilian to lowest level worker. To maximize interfaces, I visited my assigned ship on all three shifts. At the time I was assigned to a ship that had slipped its schedule for completion (upgrades and repair) two years. Pessimists doubted I would make a difference, as "my" World War II destroyer was to be transferred to an "unimportant" South American country. Thus, I confronted an unspoken, perhaps unconscious, low-priority mindset by the civilian shipyard employees. Quietly returning to the shipyard on an early-morning midnight work-shift, a worker whispered, "Lieutenant, this ship will never be overhauled completely and tested on sea trials because the ship's service generator is being ignored!"

Over the next couple of days, I discreetly affirmed that the supervisor chain was, in fact, not being truthful in their reporting. Despite reports to the contrary, the generator needed service or else the upcoming sea trials would be jeopardized and the destroyer's upgrade delayed again. If the shipyard civilian supervision staff were untruthful on the generator, I wondered how else they were misleading. Worried, I carefully considered best next steps.

First, I quietly reported, and my commander promised to check into the matter. Soon, he called me to his office to assure me that the generator repair was on schedule. As I feared, the civilian staff were being misleading or, worse, corrupt. Tactfully, I announced, "Commander, when we fail to meet the date for sea trials, please remember that I warned of this!" Shortly after, I was again called to the commander's office, "Lieutenant, you reported correctly that some of the civilian staff are lying to us. I've taken steps to ensure such fabrication stops. You double-check, but I assure you the generator will now get the attention you reported it needed." Indeed, the generator issue was being addressed, but this wasn't the only issue.

I listened. My commander doubted me at first but in the end trusted me enough to listen. Listening is a critical leader skill. Decades later, this was affirmed in my researching to identify basic leader (and follower) skills. However, listening is not the only basic skill needed for outstanding communication. Many of the other skills presented in Chapter 2's lessons play a key role in being an outstanding communicator. Perhaps as important as communication and the leader skills, are personality and values.

Before knowledge was widespread regarding my supervisor's intervention on the generator, I used the issue for further corrective action. I wanted lower-level improvement in truthfulness in regularly scheduled work progress/status meetings. Early afternoon at the end of each week, I was required to attend a "progress report meeting" regarding my ship. These were boring and maybe filled with additional false reporting that "All is well." I agonized over how to improve the situation. I attended the next meeting along with my civilian counterpart but took immediate charge instead of having him report. I stood and asked a question, "Are there any items on our ship that are slipping schedule? What is not going well?" Hearing no negative response, I announced, "Excellent." Then, to the shock of all, I asked my counterpart, the civilian "progress-man," to complete the review, and I exited. I was tired of wasting time listening to only "All's well" reports. I needed to know about anything detrimental to ship readiness.

At the next week's meeting, I again took charge and reported about the "generator-readiness falsehood." I then recommended that in the future, any supervisor responsible for a critical work slippage should report it to me—in person and immediately. That is, they should *communicate*, and with timeliness. I explained that my civilian progress-man would be glad to help prepare the report of satisfactory progress. I excused myself, explaining that I needed to visit our ship and make my daily inspection of progress. In that meeting, I did note that the supervisor responsible for the false generator readiness report had been quietly replaced and without my making such a request.

In this case, the generator was repaired on schedule and passed a rigorous inspection that allowed sea trials. We proceeded with sea trials finding all systems operational, as were innumerable other repairs and upgrades on this destroyer. Supervisors and workers had gotten the message that nothing but truthful reporting would be acceptable, at least under my oversight. But, are there ever exceptions to being 100 percent truthful? A wrongful incident, which would have delayed sea trials, occurred immediately before departing. Though observed, it went unreported. In a later chapter the incident is used to consider "rightness" or "wrongness" of silence when perhaps one should speak up. Very early in my working career, I learned the importance of communication and of sound values, especially the merit of sound ethics in communication. Regardless of the strength of a plan, it's imperative that skilled personnel executing it underpin their collective efforts with worthy principles.

> *"Leadership is the capacity to translate a vision into reality."*
> —Warren Bennis

CHAPTER 2

Lesson Plans for Basic Leader/Follower Skills

I envision this book—especially its lesson plans—in the hands of participants in an event or gathering designed to learn skills or knowledge, particularly a college classroom setting. The lesson plans could, however, be modified (expanded or condensed by excerpting) for other settings such as intensive workshops, small-group seminars, or other. To get the most out of this chapter's nine lesson plans, all of the book's other content should be reviewed. Ideally, a group would do so by learning together, but also, an individual doing personal study could find the lessons and other material in this book beneficial.

Experts, for example in business or education, are often quite intentional when choosing which words, e.g., among the following, to use: *instruct, teach, train, educate, coach, facilitate,* and so forth. For some of these terms, there are meaningful differences—subtle and not so. In my discussing *skills* here, I have chosen to always use the word *train* instead of *teach.* Similarly, I use *trainee,* despite that some may prefer *student* or *learner;* I use *trainer* instead of *professor, teacher*, or *educator*; and I use *(to) train* (verb) and *training* (noun and adjective). In the lessons, there are activities where trainees are in groups and someone within the group "leads." For these, I use the term *group leader*—rather than *student leader, trainer,* or *facilitator*.

Earlier in this book, I made the argument for our considering *follower skills* as they relate to *leader skills*. Although I generally will now simply use the phrases *leader skill(s)* or *leader skill lesson plan(s)*, readers should be mindful that followers must own these skills, truly have them—or, at least appreciate them. Outstanding leaders will ensure acolytes have these same skills also!

For Use in a College Course

As presented, the nine *training* lesson plans included in this chapter introduce and instill nine basic leader *skills* in one 75-min. class per skill, with two classes per week. In each class period, groups of 4–5 trainees practice each skill for 40 min. A lesson plan could also be "stand alone" (e.g., presented to a club of business students), but ideally, it is integrated into a three-credit-hour university course. For such a course, the first five weeks (of a typical fifteen-week college course) might be devoted to *skill training*. However, the last class in those five weeks is a transitional session, before moving on to a more typical knowledge-transmission approach in the classroom. As this is a transitional session, the trainer has the opportunity to facilitate each trainee to verbally critique the adequacy of the basic nine leader skills.

Also, trainees should be reminded that leader *skills* are important, but also at play are *personality* and a leader's *values*. Why? An evil person could use these leader skills for ill purpose. And, while emphasizing the difference between skills and knowledge, the trainer should suggest opportunities for continued leader *skill development* and leadership *knowledge acquisition*. Chapter 4 is added to emphasize the critical importance of supporting skills and knowledge with sound, constructive, values that are beneficial to society, and with consideration of leader personality.

To accommodate alternative training environments, the time allotted for "team activity" in the lesson plans might be reduced from 40 min. to as little as 25 min. per class, and the session introductions might be shortened. Specific leader skills are instilled in small-group (4–5 trainees) practice sessions. Overnight homework assignments (one-page plans for self-improvement) allow trainees to garner understanding of each skill and to gain appreciation of the complexity of their overall assimilation. In *Lesson Plan 9: Thinking Critically*, students discuss the novel notion that followers also should possess the nine basic leader skills in order to be more attentive followers and to prepare for when they are called to lead. This critical-thinking activity might require more than the designated time. Likewise, the times in other lesson plans may be increased to fill a full typical 3-credit-hour course. Adjusting of time allotted for activities is permissible to tailor or customize lesson plans for other settings, e.g., a seminar or stand-alone training event.

The class's remaining ten weeks would be devoted to *knowledge-based learning*. The follow-on topics for these ten weeks might focus on *innate leader traits* such as authenticity, analytical adaptability, creativity, courage, empathy, resilience, prowess—and to further consider *personality* and *values*. Follow-on *leadership* study might include psychology of leadership, conflict resolution, leading through change, managing versus leading, building trust and respect, and coaching to improve performance.

Order for Presentation of Lessons

Lesson 1: Team Building is suggested as the first lesson, as activities of all subsequent lessons require trainees to form groups ("teams," for this lesson) for a goal-oriented purpose. To heighten a collaborative spirit within the groups, the second lesson is *Motivating* (i.e., toward goals). The order of lessons three through eight (i.e., *Delegating, Facilitating, Giving Feedback, Listening, Mentoring,* and *Planning)* is arbitrary. The ninth lesson, *Thinking Critically,* is listed last as it requires trainees to critique (i.e., think critically) the lessons before it.

Communication?

Should "Communication"—one of the three-point improvement model's elements presented in Chapter 1—be a separate "basic" leader skill? No–it is a broad, encompassing designation, which can be broken down into various skills (e.g., listening and writing). It mixes and mingles with all nine of the basic leader skills. For example, consider "motivational communication." An example of such a perspective can be seen with the well-known and respected Toastmaster's International program, which helps its members improve their communication skills while providing practice in all nine basic leader skills. Trainees should be challenged to pursue "outside" venues such as this, as well as formal and informal knowledge-based study.

"Voice" of the Trainer

The trainer assigned to deliver each lesson should use their own imagination to improve the skill training. The trainer (especially if they are an educator first and foremost) must understand the transition from a training to educating-only environment where the goal is to impart knowledge. Training requires considerable observational skill. Educating requires lecturing skill and, generally, higher-level understanding of a topic. Making the transition from educator to trainer must be appreciated and respected, and should be explained to the trainees.

Groups: Creation, Leaders, and Activities

It is the role of the trainer to direct the specific activities and the formation of the small groups, based on their understanding of what will work best for the setting and the set of trainees they are working with. I have made suggestions for activities for the small groups to work on, but the trainer should adapt or modify these to best meet the needs of the trainees. For the small groups, I envision groups of 4–5, as that size is ideal—small enough to help ensure all have a chance to participate, and large enough to bring together diverse thoughts and personalities. From my experience, because team building is such an important skill, the composition of groups should vary (as much as practical) for each of the lessons. Depending on the nature and size of the larger group, the trainer may need to assign small groups, or the trainees may be able to self-select their own groups for the activities.

In any case, because each lesson plan requires active participation from all trainees, in turn, each trainee must lead at least one of the group activities. Again, the trainer may need to pre-select the group leaders for each lesson, or trainees may be able to quickly select their leader for each activity. The primary advantages of the trainer pre-assigning group membership and leader roles, are that this can be more time-efficient and ensure that trainees have a chance to work in different teams and all have equal opportunities to lead.

"A follower shares in an influence relationship among leaders and other followers with the intent to support leaders who reflect their mutual purposes."
—Rodger Adair

LESSON 1: BUILDING TEAMS	
	DESCRIPTION
Session Introduction (15 min.)	Explain: "Team building includes: 1) Goal alignment, 2) Building relationships, 3) Shrinking role ambiguity, and 4) Problem solving. Attaining these can require months of practice."
Group Activity (40 min.)	Assign activities from, or from a source similar to, those in the book *101 Team Building Exercises: To Improve Cooperation and Communication.**
Group Report (10 min.)	Ask each group leader to summarize their group's experience performing the assigned activity to the full group of trainees.
Assignment & Questions (10 min.)	Ask each trainee to prepare a one-page plan for self-improvement in *Team Building* to be handed in at the start of the next lesson.
Key Idea(s)	Through group activity, trainees are introduced to the skill of *Team Building* and are encouraged to continue improvement in this area.

---

* One online resource for activities is https://www.sessionlab.com/blog/team-building-activities/#awareness-circle.

LESSON 2: MOTIVATING	
	DESCRIPTION
Session Introduction (15 min.)	Explain: "Success is aided by a worthy vision achieved with communication and a sound plan. But achieving it requires motivation."
Group Activity (40 min.)	Separate into groups to brainstorm and practice motivation. For possible activities see: *workshop-bank.com/motivational-activities* or something similar. Assign activities to each group and explain that each person within a group, including the group leader, must take a turn leading one of the motivational activities.
Group Report (10 min.)	Ask each group leader to summarize their group's experience performing the assigned activity to the full group of trainees.
Assignment & Questions (10 min.)	Ask each trainee to prepare a one-page plan for self-improvement in *Motivating* to be handed in at the start of the next lesson.
Key Idea(s)	Through group activity, trainees are introduced to the skill of *Motivating* and are encouraged to continue improvement in this area.

LESSON 3: DELEGATING	
	DESCRIPTION
Session Introduction (15 min.)	Explain: "Delegating is entrusting work to another. The goal of delegation is to empower and facilitate worker/trainee effort."
Group Activity (40 min.)	Prepare and provide lists of tasks that would be appropriate to delegate. "Tasks" might include items such as 1) Persuade teammates to go on a hike, 2) Organize a farewell party for a retiring professor, 3) Buy a housewarming gift for a friend, (etc.). Explain the importance of giving some details and direction when delegating. Delegating is most successful when key information is provided but the one being delegated to has some leeway to do it their way. Distribute lists to groups and explain that, when called on to do so, the group leader will read a task aloud and assign a team member to practice delegating that task to another team member. (The person being delegated to doesn't need to perform the task, but should ask for more details if anything is unclear.)
Group Report (10 min.)	Ask each group leader to summarize their group's experience performing the assigned activity to the full group of trainees.
Assignment & Questions (10 min.)	Ask each trainee to prepare a one-page plan for improving their *Delegating* skill and to hand it in at the start of the next lesson.
Key Idea(s)	Through group activity, trainees are introduced to the skill of *Delegating* and are encouraged to continue improvement in this area.

LESSON 4: FACILITATING	
	DESCRIPTION
Session Introduction (15 min.)	Explain: "This session focuses on social facilitation as opposed to organizational, ecological, neural, and criminal facilitation. Social facilitation is a phenomenon in which being in the presence of others improves individual task performance."
Group Activity (40 min.)	Explain that each group leader is to direct their teammates to draw a "group" cartoon of their trainer. Each group member is to draw a portion of the cartoon. If the cartoon is completed quickly, improved versions should be drawn in the same manner.
Group Report (10 min.)	Ask each group leader to summarize their group's experience performing the assigned activity to the full group of trainees.
Assignment & Questions (10 min.)	Ask each trainee to prepare a one-page plan for self-improvement in *Facilitation* to be handed in at the start of the next lesson.
Key Idea(s)	Through group activity, trainees are introduced to the skill of *Facilitating* and are encouraged to continue improvement in this area.

LESSON 5: GIVING FEEDBACK	
	DESCRIPTION
Session Introduction (15 min.)	Explain: "Preliminary discussion or inquiry aids framing constructive feedback, and it is good to ask a pertinent question, or questions, and listen for an opportunity to reinforce any positive response(s). Instead of being mistake or mis-performance focused, try to suggest future goals. To avoid being defensive, circumvent negative feedback such as blurting out, 'You are wrong!' Positive feedback improves relationships, but not necessarily efficiency, and so, limit it to that which is changeable."
Group Activity (40 min.)	Direct trainees to take turns giving group members feedback regarding poor performance on items such as 1) Being late for a dinner meeting, 2) Ignoring the due date for their part of a cooperative class assignment, 3) Failing to listen to a plea to stop using foul language, 4) Being cell-phone fixated instead of trainer attentive, or 5) "Other" (similar examples).
Group Report (10 min.)	Ask each group leader to summarize their group's experience performing the assigned activity to the full group of trainees.
Assignment & Questions (10 min.)	Ask each trainee to prepare a one-page plan for self-improvement in *Giving Feedback* to be handed in at the start of the next lesson.
Key Idea(s)	Through group activity, trainees are introduced to the skill of *Giving Feedback* and are encouraged to continue improvement in this area.

LESSON 6: LISTENING	
	DESCRIPTION
Session Introduction (15 min.)	Explain: "Active listening is vital for avoiding conflict and for conflict resolution. Poor listening invites interruption, inattention, focusing on a response (i.e., instead of listening) and closed-mindedness. Active listening is an important communication skill for cultivating relationships."
Group Activity (40 min.)	Each trainee will have a turn to talk for about three minutes on a topic of their own choosing. After a trainee talks, the other group members will take turns to 1) paraphrase what they heard the speaker say and 2) ask one follow-up question to gain more information on the topic. (For this exercise, the speaker does not need to answer each question.) Once all trainees have paraphrased what they heard and asked a follow-up question for the first speaker, another trainee takes their turn as the speaker. The group leader should keep track of time, allowing for about 8–10 minutes per speaker.
Group Report (10 min.)	Ask each group leader to summarize their group's experience performing the assigned activity to the full group of trainees.
Assignment & Questions (10 min.)	Ask each trainee to prepare a one-page plan for self-improvement in *Listening* to be handed in at the start of the next lesson.
Key Idea(s)	Through group activity, trainees are introduced to the skill of *Listening*; and, are encouraged to continue improvement in this area.

LESSON 7: MENTORING	
	DESCRIPTION
Session Introduction (15 min.)	Explain: "Mentoring influences growth and requires skill in giving feedback. Mentoring includes the ideas of accompanying, sowing, catalyzing, showing, and harvesting. Studying each of these ideas will *not* occur in this lesson."
Group Activity (40 min.)	Have trainees in turn mentor their teammates on one of five topics related to "How to Prepare for Success." Assign topics to each group: 1) Schedule time, 2) Allow time to study at your pace, 3) Get rest, 4) Silence your cell phone and place it out of sight, and 5) Relax.
Group Report (10 min.)	Ask each group leader to summarize their group's experience performing the assigned activity to the full group of trainees.
Assignment & Questions (10 min.)	Ask each trainee to prepare a one-page plan for self-improvement in *Mentoring* to be handed in at the start of the next lesson.
Key Idea(s)	Through group activity, trainees are introduced to the skill of *Mentoring* and are encouraged to continue improvement in this area.

LESSON 8: PLANNING	
	DESCRIPTION
Session Introduction (15 min.)	Explain: "In the workplace, planning requires choosing a destination and best route there. For complex projects use the Critical Path Method.[†] A plan is split into key activities, each with individual start/stop times. Your group is to critique and expand on a list of activities for how to choose a college."
Group Activity (40 min.)	Provide each group with a copy of the list, which includes the following activities: 1) Develop a list of schools, 2) Narrow the list (based on affordability, reputation, student experiences, extracurricular opportunities, etc.), and 3) Reach out (to professors, students, teachers, etc.).
Group Report (10 min.)	Ask each group leader to summarize their group's experience performing the assigned activity to the full group of trainees.
Assignment & Questions (10 min.)	Ask each trainee to prepare a one-page plan for self-improvement in *Planning* skill and to hand it in at the start of the next lesson.
Key Idea(s)	Through group activity, trainees are introduced to the skill of *Planning* and are encouraged to continue improvement in this area.

† https://en.wikipedia.org/wiki/Critical_path_method.

LESSON 9: THINKING CRITICALLY	
	DESCRIPTION
Session Introduction (15 min.)	Explain: "Critical thinking considers facts, evidence, and arguments. The goal is rational, skeptical, and unbiased analyses and evaluation. Critical thinking challenges a person's (or a group's) intellectual ability, and requires pursuit of meticulous standards of excellence. Critical thinking encourages problem solving and consideration of the perspective of others regardless of differences from one's own outlook."
Group Activity (40 min.)	Each team discusses each of the nine key leader skills and ranks them by importance.
Group Report (10 min.)	In turn, choose a spokesperson from each team to summarize their team's performance in executing the activity.
Assignment & Questions (10 min.)	For homework (or self-study), each trainee chooses a prominent leader (current or historical) and rates the leader's proficiency in each of the nine key leader skills.
Key Idea(s)	Through group activity, trainees are introduced to the skill of *Thinking Critically* and are encouraged to continue improvement in this area.

"The growth and development of people is the highest calling of leadership."
—Harvey S. Firestone

CHAPTER 3

Organizational Structure

The climate in which leader skills are applied is important. Understanding one's organizational culture is wise for determining how, or even if, to practice one or more of the basic leader skills. Having had the opportunity to work in a few different organizational cultures, I share some of my experiences and insights from them.

Upon graduating with a degree in engineering (BSME), I felt too immature to immediately enter the civilian workforce. I reasoned that military experience would be the quickest path to acquire the maturity for working in business or industry. The Navy's Engineering Duty Officer (EDO) program seemed the best fit for additional technical education; I qualified because of my engineering degree. Soon I graduated from the Navy's Officer Candidate School (OCS) in Rhode Island. Fearing underwater submarine duty, I passed on an invitation to serve in Admiral Rickover's "Nuclear Navy."

Instead, I was surprised when my first assignment as an engineering duty officer was not to a shipyard but to a destroyer based in Norfolk, Virginia. I discovered this was simply part and parcel of an EDO's training, and what incredible training it turned out to be. Most interesting was that the typical line officers in the Navy were not aware of the much smaller EDO corps. Indeed, it was only through a casual tip by an engineering-school teaching assistant that I had learned about the EDO corps.

Autocratic, Top-Down "Command Control"

Though OCS tried, it didn't fully instill in me autocratic management thinking. In times of *in extremis* (extreme danger), I had no difficulty barking out an autocratic order. However, rare were the times when this harsh conduct was needed. I treated even the lowest-rated enlisted sailors with utmost respect. Amazingly, my enlisted subordinates returned the respect many times over by performing admirably for me and their ship. Indeed, I was very proud that when I needed to give a snappy, critical order, their respect and performance was astounding.

Unfortunately, one of our more senior officers subscribed to a "harsh always" interpretation of command control—that is, controlling through commands spoken with commanding voices, tones, and attitudes. He felt it was an officer's duty to show toughness in all interfaces with lower-ranked officers, and he felt it was doubly so for the non-officer enlisted. My softer approach in leading displeased him. On one occasion, I had the in-port deck watch, which was normally assigned to the least senior officers. In my bit-more-senior officer's eyes, the manner in which I requested a seaman on watch to execute a task was "too polite." Instead of taking me aside, he chastised me in front of the non-officer enlisted crew present. Dutifully, I snapped to attention and responded emphatically, "Yes, sir! You are absolutely correct!"

Pleased with his subordinate officer's acceptance of authority, the more senior officer departed, which left me alone with the enlisted personnel on watch. As soon as the senior officer was out of hearing range, I turned to the seaman and addressed him in the respectful manner as before and repeated my request. The seaman responded dutifully. More importantly, all the enlisted personnel on board our ship must have heard about the incident. Thereafter, their show of respect was extraordinary, especially in the presence of other officers.

Yes, there are occasions, in military or civilian life, when autocratic command control is necessary. However, I realized there never is an occasion when respect should be neglected, ignored, or foregone. By exercising respect over a long life, I've repeatedly been rewarded with responses showing sincere appreciation for it. Yes, there are rare occasions when individuals seem to not be able to manage respectful conduct. But when faced with these rare situations of disrespect, I try very hard not to sink to rewarding disrespect with disrespect.

Democratic, Participative Management Climates

Participative Management is democratic and collaborative. In participatory management we empower members of a group to engage in decision-making and/or a task's execution. As an adult, this leadership style seemed natural to me. Often, I wondered if it was an innate trait, or, was it learned. Perhaps it was partly because of my participation in scouting. Maybe it came through team sports.

In the 1990s, working for the federal government at one of its national research centers, a change in site directors resulted in a slow drift from TQM-oriented, participative management systems back to a hierarchical, top-down management mindset. Though I could see our organization slipping from a participative organizational style, for a while longer, process-improvement teams were permitted to form. In this period, I was approached by three electricity-savvy site-maintenance engineers. They weren't electrical engineers but were very smart when it came to civil and mechanical engineering. They requested I facilitate a team they were forming.

These folks wanted to improve the onsite electrical grid system but didn't have the funds to hire an external electrical engineering consulting firm to execute the analysis. Evidently, "my" team members didn't have appreciation for my role as facilitator. I sensed they viewed me as a command-control, give-direction-only leader rather than a same-level participant whose only purpose was to facilitate, not to "boss." Realizing their flawed perception, and thinking of the three elements (vision, plan, communication) in my model for improvement, I politely asked, "Okay, folks, what is it you wish to accomplish?" As soon as I helped my team members state the vision for their project, I asked, "How do you want to go about accomplishing your vision?"

Soon my team decided the tasks that needed to be done. As quickly, I facilitated their deciding who should do specific key tasks, including writing the summary report. The result was a first-class, engineering-team report offering a technical solution and including a budget. As the project was near completion, one of the members commented that our report was superior—at no cost, compared to the million-dollar expense of contracting the work out to a consultant.

Return to Autocratic Structure

Within the center where I was working, my skill at facilitating became more known than I realized. One day my boss's boss approached me. I was requested to facilitate a team being formed to improve our center's communications. I asked if I could reflect an hour or so and then give my answer. Attentive to the center's new director moving us back to autocratic management, I debated. I feared the more autocratic atmosphere really wasn't so interested in improving communications: When orders were given, they seemed to be blindly followed because even constructive comments were frowned upon. "Yes," I thought, "The manner of giving direction influences whether and how feedback is given."

Deciding that I shouldn't respond negatively and that perhaps I could have a constructive organizational influence, I visited my boss's boss and agreed to facilitate the team. I got right to work: The first session was scheduled only one week out, and so I scrambled to make an introductory presentation to summarize the challenge of improving organizational communication. Doing quick research on the topic, I prepared a ten-minute presentation outlining our challenge and designed to allow facilitated group interaction afterward. I assumed the team, my audience, would be composed of a mixture of leaders and non-supervisory colleagues interested in "improved center communication."

With twenty-five managers/leaders attending, I began my introductory presentation, using an overhead projector to show images on a screen. A flip chart was standing by for documenting comments made during the facilitating that was to follow. Within a minute of my presentation's start, I was interrupted by one of the managers, "When are we going to commence work on communications?" Before I could answer, my boss's boss added, "Yes, let's get started!"

What to do? Well, I responded, "Yes, let's do!" I asked, "How do you wish to proceed?" I stood by the flip chart ready to jot down their ideas for the session and to allow discussion if wanted. Soon one of them made a suggestion. I exclaimed, "Excellent!" I then pulled an image from the ones I had prepared and asked, "Is this what you are suggesting?" I was greeted with silence.

I then asked for a second idea and one was volunteered. I wrote it on the flip chart beneath the first. I pulled up a different image I had prepared, one which detailed the second suggestion, and asked, "Does this amplify your suggestion?" I was greeted with silence. Not hearing further responses, I repeated, "Other thoughts?" None forthcoming, I turned to my backup facilitator and announced so all could hear, "Maria, please stay in case these folks wish further facilitation today. If needed, I'll be in my nearby office." Picking up my presentation materials, I exited.

The next morning, I visited my boss's boss announcing, "If you folks need additional facilitated sessions, Maria will be glad to help you. I hope you folks have the best of success in improving our center's communication processes," and not wanting to again be confronted with silence or an awkward moment, I exited. Sadly, the team leaders must have decided against further efforts to improve communications, as that first "improve center communications" session was the last. Autocracy ruled.

Evaluating Leaders

Regardless of organizational structure, it is important that leadership be evaluated. Further, as well as leaders, it is as important to evaluate followers. In the previous chapter, the importance of basic leader-follower skills was introduced as well as lesson plans for instilling them. The following table is designed to evaluate either a leader's or a follower's proficiency in the nine suggested basic skills.

SKILLS ASSESSMENT: LEADING OR FOLLOWING			
Name & date:	Never	Some-times	Always
Builds Teams: Seizes opportunity for positive feedback and inspiring, value-centered conduct.			
Delegates: First acquires resources. Divides work into manageable tasks and assigns work while giving clear expectations. Steps aside but alertly monitors progress.			
Facilitates: Clarifies without being dictatorial. Stresses team effort. Encourages communication and problem solving. Stays neutral while managing dissent.			
Gives Feedback: Calmly. Action, not personality focused. Tactfully explains effect of misbehavior on others. Asks for comments and clarification. Gives examples of what is done well. Encourages at end.			
Listens: Attentively and respectfully reacts to input. Doesn't interrupt. Maintains eye contact. Summarizes to ensure understanding. Asks questions to ensure understanding.			
Mentors: Identifies persons to mentor (to improve skill, growth, and advancement potential). Always tactful, sensitive.			

Motivates: Inspires a sense of purpose, individual improvement, teaming, and lofty values. Generously gives positive feedback.			
Plans: Sets clear goals/objectives. Engages others. Identifies activities including timetables and deadlines for these.			
Thinks Critically: Gets facts first for weighing beliefs—no snap judgments. Respects opinions. Enjoys finding solutions. Doesn't fear problems and identifies/discusses them.			
Date: Completed by:			

"To me, leadership is about encouraging people. It's about stimulating them. It's about enabling them to achieve what they can achieve—and to do that with a purpose."
—Christine Lagarde

CHAPTER 4

Additional Considerations:
Leader Personality and Values

What's your personality? How about your values? This chapter is not designed to instill a new skill. Rather, it suggests inculcation through large group discussion, as well as self-discernment and appreciation, that acquiring Chapter 2's nine leader skills are not an "end all." This chapter's purpose is to underscore the contention that understanding the complexity of leading deserves future study for what I may have overlooked. For example, it was only long after I developed the nine basic leader skills that I learned it might be wise to consider leader *personality* and *values*.

Personality

Most psychologists suspect personality is innate/genetic rather than learned. Many have strived to classify personality characteristics into five main categories referred to as the "Big Five personality traits" shown here and as summarized on Wikipedia: For each, a person's personality could be placed on a continuum, between "very" and "not at all."

- Openness to Experience *(inventive/curious vs. consistent/ cautious)*
- Conscientiousness *(efficient/organized vs. extravagant/ careless)*
- Extroversion *(outgoing/energetic vs. solitary/reserved)*
- Agreeableness *(friendly/compassionate vs. critical/judgmental)*
- Neuroticism *(sensitive/nervous vs. resilient/confident)*

Values

In my early Total Quality Management (TQM) training, values were stressed. We would form TQM teams and a first step was to agree upon and set team values. This caused personal agony as it forced me to think about my own key values; or, at least what they should be.

I quietly debated for weeks, "What should my two or three key values be?" One day I realized they had been right in front of me for years. Since childhood, in my church the priest directed us to use three essential values as we went forward to receive Communion. However, daydreaming in Sunday service, I never truly digested these values. Years later, one Sunday, while daydreaming about the private sector values I needed to discover and adopt for my then total-quality-oriented workplace, I heard and was given to understand them. I took in—perhaps, truly for the first time—the call to Communion, "In fear of God, with faith and love come forward." For years I wondered why one should be "fearful" to accept Communion. My aunt Sarah refused to just wonder about this wording. She asked our clerical leader, who explained that it actually meant go forward "in awe of God," which means respectfully. In the most bizarre way, I was gifted with the values *respect, faith, and love*. Thereafter, Respect—Faith—Love became a trinity of my primary values. Only in the last few years did I decide a fourth value was needed, "truth." Now my trinity of values is supported by a fourth, *truthfulness*.

A Sampling of Values

Accomplishment	Dignity	Inspiration	Restraint
Accountability	Discipline	Integrity	Reverence
Accuracy	Effectiveness	Intelligence	Rigor
Achievement	Efficiency	Joy	Risk
Adaptability	Empathy	Justice	Satisfaction
Altruism	Enthusiasm	Kindness	Security
Ambition	Equality	Knowledge	Self-reliance
Awareness	Ethicalness	Learning	Selflessness
Balance	Excellence	Liberty	Sensitivity
Beauty	Experience	Logic	Service
Boldness	Exploration	Love	Sharing
Bravery	Fairness	Loyalty	Significance
Brilliance	Fearlessness	Mastery	Simplicity
Calm	Fidelity	Meaning	Sincerity
Care	Focus	Moderation	Skillfulness
Challenge	Foresight	Motivation	Solitude
Clarity	Fortitude	Openness	Spirituality
Commitment	Freedom	Optimism	Stability
Common sense	Friendship	Order	Stewardship
Compassion	Fun	Organization	Strength
Competence	Generosity	Originality	Success
Connection	Gratitude	Passion	Support
Consistency	Growth	Patience	Sustainability
Contentment	Hard work	Peace	Teamwork
Contribution	Harmony	Persistence	Thoroughness
Conviction	Honesty	Playfulness	Thoughtfulness
Cooperation	Honor	Potential	Timeliness
Courage	Hope	Productivity	Tolerance
Creativity	Humility	Professionalism	Tranquility
Credibility	Humor	Purpose	Transparency
Curiosity	Imagination	Quality	Trust
Decisiveness	Improvement	Realism	Truthfulness
Dedication	Independence	Reason	Understanding
Dependability	Individuality	Recognition	Unity
Development	Innovation	Respect	Vitality
Devotion	Insight	Responsibility	Wisdom

Of course, simply *having* a value isn't good enough; one must also know when and how to *use* that value. I recall an incident from my US Navy days when what it meant to be truthful was put to the test, with silence winning the day. When is remaining silent critical? Can silence be an act of truthfulness? As the WWII destroyer described in Chapter 1 left for sea trials, the ship's commander gave the order to cast off the lines that anchored our ship to the pier. In shock, I observed this being done incorrectly. The borrowed, reserve-fleet deck crew cast off the lines incorrectly. The lines were left tied to the pier and were not hauled onto our ship. Without the lines, it would be difficult (if not impossible) to port the ship in any other location than the pier we just left. I debated, what to do? If I reported the mistake, it would delay sailing by hours as the process of retrieving the lines would have been a bit complicated and embarrassing for the borrowed crew.

I reasoned that we would return to the same pier after sea trials. Just before returning, I could call the shipyard to have men standing by to throw us the lines from shoreside. Not my direct responsibility, if we had been required to dock in another location, I would share no blame for the missing lines. What would be my most truthful action? Would it be silence in order to give our mission, sea trials, highest priority? Would it be to delay sea trials to retrieve the ropes inappropriately lying on the pier? What would you have done? The point in sharing this silent dilemma is that deciding the most "truthful" action sometimes can be challenging.

From Skills to Knowledge in the Classroom

My leader skill lessons are designed to instill nine skills, one lesson per skill. Each trainee is given the opportunity to actively demonstrate each skill through small group activities. This differs from the typical knowledge-based school environment. However, we must not dismiss the importance of knowledge-only instruction. In this regard, the present chapter transitions to the more typical knowledge-transmission approach, with a goal of ensuring participant awareness of topics such as leader values and the surprisingly few categories for personality traits.

Where we get our personality and values, and how they do—or do not—develop over time, are complicated questions. At the risk of over-simplifying, for the purposes of this text, I'll say that personality is generally innate, whereas values are mostly learned. This means personality is something of a constant that we have to work with, whereas there is significant potential to teach, instill, and develop values. Regardless, mutual appreciation of these is important for both followers and leaders.

Thus, the class members should be invited to reflect on which of "The Big Five" personality traits they possess. The class should also be asked which two or three values are central to how they approach their life and work. This provides the opportunity for the instructor to put on an educator's hat. It provides the chance for the instructor to explain the transition to sit-and-listen, knowledge-based educating.

Another exercise might be a collective thought experiment with the class. The instructor might select a handful of historical personalities, each paired with a brief biographical sketch. The class might then speculate on values and personalities of each historical person. The class might also explore how these elements would have played a role in the challenges the historical figures faced.

This is also an opportunity to spend some time reflecting on how personality and values affect how the nine leader/follower skills are expressed. For instance, how does *giving feedback* look different between someone who is introverted and values peace, as compared to someone who is extroverted and values honesty?

To continue the theme of thinking critically from Lesson 9, this is a good time to step back and evaluate the adequacy of the nine skills presented in the lessons. Are any of those nine non-essential? Are there any fundamental skills missing?

This chapter's discussion has largely been abstract, theoretical. The following two chapters, however, give us a chance to think about pursuing improvement in more specific contexts.

> ## "When your values are clear to you, making decisions becomes easier."
> —Roy E. Disney

CHAPTER 5

Your Belief's Improvement Model?

Like all large secular organizations (government or business), all religious communities have models of governance, written or not. These generally include both ordained and lay participants. Regardless of community structure, there is abundant potential for failure of visioning, planning, or communicating. As in the secular world, sight of destination, of the true vision of destination, is needed. A strategy to achieve the vision is needed. A sound plan is necessary. The communication processes are vital to ensure all work in concert to achieve the collective vision. Vision, plan, and communication—when considered and executed with strong leadership and followership—are the major ingredients for individual and collective improvement in a religion or in the secular domain.

The Challenges before Us

In my varied exposure to a diversity of religions, too often we witness the lack the leadership talent to support continuous improvement. Compounding our challenge, too often we give inadequate attention to the basic individual leader skills needed to support our major organizational goals. For example, this is the selection of the basic skills proposed in Chapter 2: *Building Teams, Delegating, Facilitating, Giving Feedback, Listening, Mentoring, Motivating Planning,* and *Critical Thinking.* Many times, we casually pass management and execution of organizational goals to our leader of the moment without realizing we each must have these skills to be good followers *and* for when it is our turn to lead.

In most belief systems, we are encouraged to recognize our fallibilities, pray for forgiveness of them, and improve because of them. Also important, is learning how to manage the failings of our leaders. Instead of quietly castigating them for mistakes, it's vital we understand a leader's fallibility in order to deliver constructive feedback for their improvement. The evaluation form featured in Chapter 3 shows one approach for giving feedback in the spirit of helping a person improve. The form is valid for all, leader or follower, and should be undertaken with an understanding of the community leadership structure, as addressed in Chapter 3.

I suspect research would determine similar improvement challenges within all religious traditions, including but not limited to Christianity, Islam, Judaism, Buddhism, and Hinduism. Managing our human frailness, our fallibility, is a universal challenge. It would be fascinating to uncover, in simplest terms, models for improvement most appropriate for each tradition; or, if such a pursuit is inconsequential to a specific faith. I suspect that my simplified model for organization improvement and my belief of just nine basic leader skills may be a too unique a notion, a too great simplification. If so, I pray that my assertions relative to an organizational improvement model and leader skillfulness are challenged and improved.

Focusing on Growth

I confess that, previously in life, I was deficient regarding the need to identify and apply (in a more rigorous manner) the key attributes of my faith. I suspect, like many members of my faith, I took these for granted. I participated in the rituals of a Christian upbringing. However, I wanted more than ritual. I reasoned the value of Christianity was our continuous growth—individually through our faith, and together through our living and sharing of it. Reaching this conclusion, I set out to contribute to the cause of improvement by using skills and knowledge available to me— project engineering and a cursory understanding of developing training materials / seminars. Also, I was building upon my experiences. This was a time well before I developed and settled on the "vision, plan, and communication" model for improvement.

I had a vision for my specific church community. We would grow our "too small" congregation. Empty pews were discomforting I thought. I became fixated on growth, perhaps to too great a degree. My vision became, "Grow membership." I also had a plan, which was simple and two-pronged. First, I would dedicate my creative engineering skills to the physical improvement of our church facilities. By doing so, I thought I would gain sufficient appreciation from our members such that they would join me in a new initiative to promote our growth in numbers. I envisioned our eventually working together to fill our many empty pews. For several years, I applied my creativity and project management skills to leading initiatives for church "building projects." I worked patiently while contemplating the best time to promote growth in membership.

During this period, I was familiarized with the concepts of facilitated training. So, to enhance my eventual pitch for our church's growth in membership, I introduced training to reinforce collaborative effort and minimum command-control tendencies. I designed and led two training-type, all-day Saturday workshops to impart collaborative skills to underpin a growth-in-numbers initiative. To enhance a spirit of growth, I envisioned teamwork as critical. The workshops emphasized facilitated team activities and the importance of inclusion. The two workshops minimized lecturing and maximized small, working group activities. I was encouraged that a significant accomplishment of the workshops was a marked increase of mutual respect among participants. A more respectful, inclusive, cooperative climate emerged in this group of congregants.

Though the physical improvements to our facilities and the two workshops were successful, I realized mere respect for what I had contributed was insufficient to bring about interest in my ideas for congregational growth. I faced a most disappointing failure. I was unable to persuade any other person, not one, in our congregation to support the concept of growing our numbers. I was unable to cause our clerical leader to retreat from a command-control mindset to a participative one and join me in the process of helping our congregation rethink its obligation to support growth. I failed to underpin interest in growth with the requirement of the New Testament passage "... where two or three are gathered." No single other member of our small congregation, including our clerical leader, would join me in a growth movement.

Despite my numerous contributions toward our improvement, I didn't have enough stature in the eyes of our members to be heeded in my plea for growth. And, I came to learn my weakness might be communication, especially "salesmanship-related communication," including reading my audience. When one attempts to introduce a major change in thinking—a change in mindset—they are an influencer, which can be exciting but also hard. And, personality certainly comes into play. I came to realize how complex and great the challenge is when introducing change.

There seemed to be a quiet, perhaps subconscious, fear-based feeling toward the idea of growing our membership, yet I truly felt that we needed to change, and to look beyond the comforts and familiarity of remaining small. In time I would learn that the few new members of our congregation felt it took too long to feel welcomed, which was a bit of useful information.

New Conversations and Questions

After considering my next steps (I wasn't going to give up), I specifically requested our clerical leader's support in persuading the rest of the congregation that growing our membership was important. I reasoned that he, our spiritual leader, being schooled within a command-control leadership environment, was not attuned to the participative approaches needed to accommodate my ideas for how to grow. My interest in growth was steered away from our local church: He suggested a church conference on the West Coast of our country and handed me a brochure. He indicated that the people who were leading and would attend the gathering were the wing of our faith interested in church growth. My contributing to physical improvements of local church property was accepted; however, my desires for and concept of outreach to garner support for our church's growth in numbers were not.

Heeding my clerical leader's recommendation, I attended the conference. In doing so, I gained a better understanding of a rare group in our faith interested in and knowledgeable about the nuances of church growth. This group was made up of outreach-minded folks who had converted to our sect of the Christian faith. Soon, I found myself in a small group meeting set up for a few folks (5–6 from the approximately 400 conference attendees) who were facing membership challenges similar to my church's. I was confronted with a surprising discussion of the challenge. We learned that congregations with fewer than one hundred members were seldom interested in growth.

Regarding efforts to convert other Christians to their branch of our faith, potential converts were more accepted in congregations with more than one hundred members. Small congregations tended to have an introverted personality and often felt uncomfortable embracing new (i.e., different) people and ideas. The "beware of strangers" attitude was typical in these smaller churches. In large congregations, numerous cells with varied interests form. Thus, a newcomer is more likely to find a place to fit in—that is, a small group of folks with similar interests and needs.

With this understanding that smallness wants to stay small, my hope for growing my church's membership was crushed. However, I had developed a simplified secular model for improvement and thought perhaps at this conference I might discover the Church's similar model for improvement if such existed.

I thought maybe my secondary personal-agenda topic should be shared. Therefore, summoning up the courage, I sought out the respected conference leader, who invited me to sit with him a few minutes at a conference table during one of our session breaks. Again, summoning up my courage, I asked permission to share a 5-minute notebook presentation titled, "Simplified Model for Our Improvement." He listened attentively as I quickly flipped notebook pages and ended with my model. I was flattered that such a leader allowed me this invaluable time. I displayed the next-to-last graphic, my three-point model for continuous improvement—Vision, Plan, and Communication. As he studied it, I asked, "What is the Church's model for our improvement?" Instead of answering, he looked up, thoughtfully announcing, "I'm going to have you speak to one of our most scholarly leaders."

A few hours later, at this religious conference in California, I was meeting with the then dean[*] of an East Coast seminary. Feeling a bit intimidated, I repeated the "Vision, Plan, and Communication" presentation to this person who had flown 3000 miles to be one of the conference's speakers. I ended my presentation by again sharing my three-point model for improvement. I asked the dean, "What is the Church's model for improvement?" Apparently, he felt this was a good question for a wider audience of believers. The dean requested I come to his college to present my concept.

At his college several weeks later, nearing the end of my slide presentation, I asked the audience of instructors and students my still-unanswered question: "What is the Church's model for improvement?" Silence followed. Interrupting the quietude, I revealed the next slide summarizing my very recent best guess of the Church's model: the Trinity—the Father, Son and Holy Spirit. I gave a brief explanation. "We are taught that salvation in Christ is the primary Christian vision. God the Father offers the plan for that salvation. The Holy Spirit communicates and provides the means for understanding God's plan for us."

In studying the Christian concept of Trinity, I saw a parallel to my "general" model. While all analogies or images of the Trinity (e.g., three leaves of a clover or three sides of a triangle) are inadequate, this thought experiment can still be useful. Each of the elements of my model are vital, but incomplete if isolated;

---

[*]   https://en.wikipedia.org/wiki/George_Dragas

they exist as a unity, given meaning and purpose by each other. A vision without a plan will not be realized. A plan needs a vision to give it structure. A vision or plan without communication will never make progress. And without a vision or plan, what is there to communicate? Although this line of thought can be helpful for Christians, my simple Vision, Plan, Communication model may be easier for a wider improvement-minded audience to appreciate. However, Christians are obligated to respect the model the Trinity represents in the way each is taught.

My presentation complete, a long silence greeted me. Was my presentation a failure? About to conclude with the standard, "I thank you for your invitation to visit," I was interrupted by a standing ovation. Yet, even with this flattering moment of approval, I received no feedback, no comment, no other reaction. Indeed, I have yet to receive affirmation or rejection of my ideas about the Church's model for improvement. Thus, I ponder, "How can Christian communion—affinity and connection—matter in a community that fails at communication?" Well, to me, it matters. But, I recognize that my expectations may be too high. The lapse may be due my personal inadequacies. The lapse may be that folks like me are not doing enough to advance and improve our discussion processes. Perhaps by being published, this work might inspire useful answers to my search for insight and simplicity that will benefit others in search of self and organizational improvement.

An Insight on Leadership

Returning to my initial observations, within the various rules and structures of governance for religious communities, fallible humans that we are, the potential for breakdown of our vision, plan, and communication is inevitable. Thus, as developed in Chapter 3, an understanding of one's organizational structure is important, whether it's autocratic, participative, or a confusion of both. And, as addressed in Chapter 4, it's important to appreciate that leader personalities vary, and can be assessed along a continuum of traits. Finally, with that background knowledge, we are then in a place to appreciate basic leadership skills, and, more importantly, understand that each of us may have an obligation to acquire these skills.

My quest to understand leader skills had begun in concern for the importance of lay leaders in my own, local church and for how to identify them. During that meeting with a well-regarded scholar of my faith mentioned previously, I had asked him a question about how we chose our leaders. He directed me to this Bible passage:

> But you are a chosen generation, *a royal priesthood*, a holy nation, His own special people, that you may proclaim the praise of Him who called you out of darkness into His marvelous light; who once were not a people but are now the people of God, who had not obtained mercy but now have obtained mercy. —1 Peter 2:9–10 (NKJV, emphasis mine)

He explained: Each of us who declares being of the Christian faith is obligated to assume some form of leader responsibility. As St. Peter declares, we are a "royal priesthood." Thus, each of us has the responsibility of a leader. At first, I was in disbelief that all had leadership obligation. In time I accepted the notion and continued to work on how to pursue improvement, beyond the foundation of my three-point model. I eventually arrived at the understanding that specific skills are required of those leading the work of improvement as well as of the followers. Thus, my nine basic leader skills are required of all people, whether leading directly or supporting the work of a leader as a follower. Also, a follower should be prepared for the day when they need to lead.

I also recalled my early experience as a youngster in Boy Scouts, in which all members were encouraged to develop leader competence—this is true in other respected youth programs too, such as 4-H and FFA. Over many, many years since, I've became preoccupied for how best to develop our leading skills in a more succinct comprehensive manner. This book shares insights regarding what leadership entails and specific basic skills needed. Yes, we most often assume the role of "follower." However, I agree with St. Peter, that each of us must prepare for our turn to lead.

In this book, my intent is not to promote Christian principles or leadership. Rather, I invite all people of all faiths to consider how some of the nine leader/follower skills presented herein are applicable to your belief, and to search for and acquire the leader/follower skills that are appropriate for your belief.

Importance of Community

In my advanced years, in a search to learn the most significant reason Christianity grew and spread, an insight came. I imagine it's quite possible that the Romans and fortuitous timing created the seedbed for that growth. When Christianity was born, Rome had conquered and subdued, or was in the process of conquering and subduing, the "known world." In so doing, the Romans, perhaps inadvertently, destroyed a sense of community in the conquered lands. This would have created a vacuum wherein the handiest means of the time to satisfy the need for community was Christianity. The Church may have offered satisfaction for this need and thus the seed of Christianity grew and flourished in virtually all the lands Rome conquered. If correct, and I believe it may be, this thesis for early church growth explains the vital need of humans for a sense a community, belonging, inclusion. Thus, in our pursuit of improvement, we should never neglect emphasizing and cultivating a sense of community (i.e., participative communication) in our endeavors, be they secular or religious.

*"The very essence of leadership
is that you have to have a vision.
It's got to be a vision you articulate
clearly and forcefully on every occasion.
You can't blow an uncertain trumpet."*
—Theodore Hesburgh

CHAPTER 6

The Work ahead of Us

I thought this book's draft was done, but a friend mentioned how our nation seems to be in peril, in need of improvement, and sorely lacking a core set of shared values. Indeed, I agreed, this might be the case. Then I wondered how this book relates to the monumental issues we face nationally. I wondered, "Could my simple model introduced in Chapter 1 be key for improvement nationally? Or is the scale of our national reality so complex my model wouldn't make a difference? Is there a superior model, and if so, what is it? Is the idea of continuous improvement a passed fad?"

As I looked at various facets of our society for positive drivers of improvement, I was reminded that there are many passionate folks in our nation who have dedicated themselves to tirelessly working for the improvement of individuals and their communities. Health-care workers and teachers come to mind. Doctors, nurses, and assistants are passionate about achieving the best results for their patients, even in the midst of significant challenges such as battling with insurance companies, concern about the bottom line from their employers, and so forth. In classrooms, teachers devote themselves to ensure their students' progress. The most important values for fueling continuous improvement are passion and caring for the vision we are pursuing.

Our Motivations

Passion and caring can lead to great results. For me, my passion is to share the nine basic leadership skills, that to date seem uniquely identified. My challenge is to inspire others to improve and refine those basic skills. My passion is to sell the vision that these skills should be instilled in all of us but especially young people. It isn't sufficient to simply describe the nine basic leader skills. Rather, as I attempted in Chapter 2, it is necessary to flesh out these kinds of ideas even more and create awareness of them. It is necessary to help people move from learning *about* these skills to persuading people to seek *training* in them, and then, to *practice* them.

Shifting from an individual to a communal focus, I wonder if there is a "shared" national passion that drives how society works in the United States. Our country's Declaration of Independence hints at one possible set of passions: our right to life, liberty, and pursuit of happiness. Too often we think of these critical values selfishly—my life, my liberty, and my happiness. Perhaps we should think of these values within the framework of a higher-level obligation, "Our life, our liberty, and our happiness." Those are noble pursuits, for sure, but I believe there is a fundamental element—a value—that needs to be in place in order for life, liberty, and happiness to flourish. In earlier chapters, the importance and quandaries of truthfulness were briefly mentioned. Perhaps, the foundational pursuits (i.e., life, liberty and happiness) engrained in us through our Declaration of Independence are most heightened with greater respect for and appreciation of the truth.

Truthfulness in Use

Without honesty as a key value practiced by our collective society, all else crumbles. To properly value the truth, we must be humble enough to recognize that we do not always see the whole picture for ourselves, and at the same time recognize our hesitancy to speak up when we witness truthfulness being discounted.

I wondered about my instincts with respect to truth within my forty-plus years of federal government employment. For example, was the importance of truthfulness sufficiently emphasized in our government—by its leaders, in policy development, in executing the government's work? I searched for evidence of interest in truthfulness. I researched and was delighted to discover the following excerpt, which was taken from the website for the US Department of Justice:

- *Independence and Impartiality.* The Justice Department works each day to earn the public's trust by following the facts and the law wherever they may lead, without prejudice or improper influence.
- *Honesty and Integrity.* The Justice Department's employees adhere to the highest standards of ethical behavior, mindful that, as public servants, we must work to earn the trust of, and inspire confidence in, the public we serve.
- *Respect.* The Justice Department's employees value differences in people and in ideas and treat everyone with fairness, dignity, and compassion.
- *Excellence.* The Justice Department works every day to provide the highest levels of service to the American people and to be a responsible steward of the taxpayers' dollars.

One can't argue with such an outstanding list of values. Truthfulness is embedded in the second bullet and is possibly required in the first. Then came to mind the oath one takes when being sworn in to testify in court:

Do you solemnly (swear/affirm) that you will tell the *truth*, the whole *truth*, and nothing but the *truth*?

The courts understand the importance of honesty, knowing full well that justice is not possible without truth, and progress cannot be made without it. The challenge is how to inspire greater interest in inspiring truthfulness in all sectors of government, the private sector workplace, in our local communities, and so forth. But, what's the plan for doing this? Or, is such an executable plan possible?

A National Model?

Through my years of studying and pursuing improvement, it's no surprise that I became familiar with the American Society for Quality (ASQ), a global organization founded in 1946. This is a highly regarded organization that does exactly what I have been advocating here: It trains individuals and institutions on how to improve their work and increase their quality in whatever they do. The difference in how I've approached the question of how to pursue improvement, compared to ASQ, is by emphasizing *simplicity*. Thus, I developed the three core elements of *vision, plan*, and *communication*, along with the nine leader skills. If there is to be a model for pursuing improvement at a national level, then surely a respected authority such as ASQ would have much to contribute. Certainly, too, there is extensive, relevant research to study and learn from. Until that time, I will continue to work with my three-point model, and show how it can shed some light on the challenge to continuously improve societal truthfulness. So, I ask, "How can vision, plan, and communication be used on such a grand, ambitious scale? What is needed of these three elements to articulate a specific, national model for improvement?" Would something like the following be the basis for a national model?

- Vision: Preserve and enhance our democratic heritage.
- Plan: With truthfulness as the foremost value, we shall document, periodically review, and apply all practical means to maintain and improve our republic.
- Communication: All citizens shall be granted opportunity to support our vision and plan for the continuous improvement of our nation, both as individuals and as communities working together.

The above example of how my model can be fleshed out for this particular context assumes that there is a team who can uphold the vision, guide the plan, and facilitate communication. All this work must rest on truth. How this happens, exactly, is not the focus of this book, but I do insist that it is of utmost importance that American citizens give such thinking attention.

An Invitation to Action

Having looked at this matter in terms of a grand (national) scale, I dare not end without inviting the reader to consider all the many different ways in which we can also work for improvement on a more modest scale—in our own lives and communities.

There is promise for using my three-point model and related skills for various arenas throughout life. For each of these, there are both individual and communal elements—a "me" and an "us." When we work toward personal improvement, we model the task for those whom we work with, and we invite them to participate in the improvements of larger systems, communities, and relationships. There's always room for improvement in close relationships of friends and families, among colleagues, in neighborhoods, in community service organizations, in local political bodies, in private business, in government and so forth.

Conceivably, when we seriously attempt to recognize the possibilities for improvement, when we commit ourselves to the work of improvement, and when we decide to own a model of improvement and use it for ourselves and beyond, great things can happen.

"Continuous improvement is better than delayed perfection."
—Mark Twain

About the Author

In 1975, while working as an engineer on US government energy projects, Tom George was awarded a Certificate of Excellence by the Society for Technical Communication. The honor did not prompt him to forsake engineering for a career in literature, but maybe it did plant a seed, because now in "retirement" Tom is writing with the same vigor he brought to his profession.

In a career spanning forty years, Tom has developed training manuals, designed and inspected aerial tramways, worked on coal gasification and liquefaction, patented two processes for improving fuel cells, and done important work in engineering cost analysis, boiler test standards, cooperative research on turbine systems, and electricity grid design. Through it all, Tom has only strengthened his commitment to quality improvement in all that he does.

Tom has also devoted much energy to community service and to advocating for sensible planning, and neighborhood preservation and restoration in his home city of Morgantown, West Virginia. Before retirement, Tom spent much of his leisure time in carpentry, online investing, hiking/backpacking, kayaking, and, of course, writing. In retirement, Tom is committed to promoting improved identification of key leader skills and how best to instill them on a sound value basis in all, but most especially young people.

Made in USA - Kendallville, IN
28588_9781733897266
12.07.2024 2055